TAURUS

This Book Belongs To

———————————————

TAURUS

The Sign of the Bull
April 21– May 21

By Teresa Celsi
and Michael Yawney

Ariel Books

Andrews and McMeel
Kansas City

TAURUS

ISBN: 0–8362–3079–5
Library of Congress Catalog Card Number: 93-73358

Contents

Astrology—An Introduction   *7*

The Sign of the Bull   *12*

Character and Personality   *14*

Signs and Symbols   *18*

Health and Fitness   *20*

Home and Family   *22*

Careers and Goals   *24*

Pastimes and Play   *26*

Love Among the Signs   *28*

Taurus with Aries   *32*

Taurus with Taurus   *36*

Taurus with Gemini   40

Taurus with Cancer   44

Taurus with Leo   48

Taurus with Virgo   52

Taurus with Libra   56

Taurus with Scorpio   60

Taurus with Sagittarius   64

Taurus with Capricorn   68

Taurus with Aquarius   72

Taurus with Pisces   76

Astrology

An Introduction

E arly in our history, as humankind
changed from hunter-gatherers
to farmers, they left the forests
and moved to the plains, where they
could raise plants and livestock. While
they guarded their animals at night,
the herders gazed up at the sky. They
watched the stars circle Earth, counted
the days between moons, and perceived
an order in the universe.

Astrology was born as a way of finding a meaningful relationship between the movements of the heavens and the events on Earth. Astrologers believe that the celestial dance of planets affects our personalities and destinies. In order to better understand these forces, an astrologer creates a chart, which is like a snapshot of the heavens at the time of your birth. Each planet—Mercury, Venus, Mars, Jupiter, Saturn, Uranus, Neptune, and Pluto—has influence on you. So does the place of your birth.

The most important element in a chart is your sun sign, commonly known as your astrological sign. There are twelve signs of the zodiac, a belt of sky encircling Earth that is divided into twelve zones. Whichever zone the sun was in at your time of birth determines your sun sign. Your sun sign influences conscious behavior. Your moon sign influences unconscious behavior. (This book deals only with sun signs. To find your moon sign, you must look in a reference book or consult an astrologer.)

Each sign is categorized under one of the four elements: *fire*, *earth*, *air*, or *water*. Fire signs (Aries, Leo, and Sagittarius) are creative and somewhat self-centered. Earth signs (Taurus, Virgo, and Capricorn) are steady and desire material things. Air signs (Gemini, Libra, and Aquarius) are clever and intellectual.

Water signs (Cancer, Scorpio, and Pisces) are emotional and empathetic.

Each sign has one of three qualities—*cardinal*, *fixed*, or *mutable*—which shows how it operates. Cardinal signs (Aries, Cancer, Libra, and Capricorn) use their energy to lead in a direct, forceful way. Fixed signs (Taurus, Leo, Scorpio, and Aquarius) harness energy and use it to organize and consolidate. Mutable signs (Gemini, Virgo, Sagittarius, and Pisces) use energy to transform and change.

Every sign has a different combination of an element and a quality. When the positions of all the twelve planets are added to a chart, you can begin to appreciate the complexity of each individual. Astrology does not simplify people by shoving them into twelve personality boxes; rather, the details of your chart will be amazingly complex, inspiring the same awe those early herders must have felt while gazing up into the mystery of the heavens.

The Sign of the Bull

The sign of Taurus is symbolized by the bull. One of the first domesticated animals, the bull became important with the emergence of agriculture. When humankind stopped roaming and hunting and settled into communities to raise crops and animals, the bull became increasingly vital to their growth and success. Thus the bull is key to the creation of modern civilization.

Bulls also figure heavily throughout ancient mythology. In Greek mythology, Zeus, king of the gods, occasionally assumed the form of a bull in order to seduce mortal women and thus father heroes. In this way, he wooed Europa and carried her across the sea to Crete, where her son, Minos, founded a great civilization.

Taurus's ruling planet is Venus, named after the Roman goddess of love and beauty who lured her lovers into a shady bower where they made love amid fragrant blossoms. Venus endows those born under this sign with heightened sensuality and an innate sense of beauty.

Character and Personality

T he story of Ferdinand the Bull beautifully illustrates the personality of a Taurus. Ferdinand is a gentle creature whose favorite occupation is sitting under a tree, smelling a delicate flower. He sniffs the flower, enjoying its sweet smell. But when stung by a bee, Ferdinand erupts into a snorting, savage rage. This is exactly what a Taurus is like.

Although those born under this sign have great strength, they are also gentle and patient. They are very sensual and romantic, enjoying anything they can see, touch, taste, smell, or hear. They are particularly fond of music, food, and drink.

Tauruses can also be very stubborn. When Ferdinand decides not to fight, all the matadors in the world can't change his mind. He plops right down in the middle of the bullring. It's the same for a real-life Taurus. Nothing is more immovable. Rage all you like, ignore or cajole, but once the Bull has made up its mind, that's that.

Tauruses are usually placid, but their tempers can be terrible—and they tend

15

to keep their rage bottled up until it explodes. You see, Tauruses are collectors. Once they have something, they don't want to let it go, including their feelings. Other, more extroverted sun signs will complain to let off steam; Taurus will not. Good feelings warm the Bull's heart, while bad feelings fester and grow until they burst out of the Bull like a volcano erupting. Even Taurus finds this loss of control terrifying.

Luckily, such eruptions are rare. Most Bulls live much of their lives without experiencing the depths of their rage. They are steady and docile and deeply loving, even if they are not very demonstrative.

As workers, Bulls excel. Their output is steady and always of good quality. They don't call in sick unless they're too weak to get out of bed. They meet deadlines and will work extra hours without complaint.

Tauruses also make very good lovers and friends. However, a strange shyness causes them difficulty when they try to make the first move. If you want to get to know a Taurus, take a chance and give him or her a call. You'll probably make a very faithful friend or an affectionate, giving lover.

Signs and Symbols

E ach sign in the zodiac is ruled by a different planet. Taurus is ruled by Venus, named after the goddess of love and sensuality. Taurus is symbolized by the bull, which figures in Greek mythology as the guise Zeus frequently chose so he could seduce mortal women.

Taurus combines the element of earth (sensuality) with the fixed quality of harnessed energy. Those born under this sign are powerful, effective organizers. The second sign of the zodiac, Taurus is essentially a cultivator. It is quiet, stable, patient, secure, stubborn, and loving.

Taurus is associated with Friday and rules the throat and neck. The animal associated with Taurus is, of course, the bull and all cattle. Taurus's colors are all pastels; its gemstones are emerald and moss agate; and its metal is copper. Its lucky number is six.

Plants and flowers linked with Taurus are the daisy, larkspur, rose, columbine, lily, and foxglove. Its foods are beefsteak, wheat, beans, spinach, apples, and pears.

Health and Fitness

Tauruses are generally strong enough to shake off most illnesses without breaking stride. Even when they aren't feeling well, they continue to plug along.

For this reason, they tend to recuperate very slowly when they do become sick. They aren't good at following the doctor's instructions, either. An innate pessimism keeps the Bull from believing it will get well, and just sheer stubbornness keeps it from getting worse.

The most vulnerable areas for Taurus are the throat and neck. Other sensitive areas are the legs, ankles, reproductive organs, back, and spinal cord. Sore throats and viral infections can also be nuisances to the hearty Bull.

Tauruses are also prone to gaining weight: They love to eat and hate to diet, so they need to practice moderation in eating and drinking. Exercise and plenty of fresh air will also help the sturdy Bull stay in shape.

Home and Family

If a Taurus doesn't already own a home, he or she usually wants to —and probably in the suburbs. The Bull needs to have a bit of the earth—and roots—to feel comfortable. And speaking of comfortable, that's what a Taurus home will be: well furnished, with plush cushions, deep carpets, thick towels, and a well-stocked kitchen. Bulls love to entertain in their homes, especially throwing small dinner parties.

This earth sign loves to work the soil and usually has some garden space. Even in a small apartment, a true Taurus will have a window box or a few houseplants.

Young Bulls mature quickly and can be very charming. They may have trouble controlling their tempers, though, and should be treated with patience and understanding.

Taurus mothers are good at providing a stable and emotionally supportive environment. Fathers can sometimes become too reserved and rigid for their teenagers. It may take years before children learn to appreciate their Taurus fathers.

Careers and Goals

Farming, raising plants, and breeding stock are all good occupations for this earth sign. Since Tauruses love to cook, Bulls make good chefs. Composing music, writing, drawing, and engineering take advantage of Taurus's natural artistic ability.

Tauruses are best when working alone, so they can concentrate. Meetings distract them, and they don't feed well off other people's energy. Bulls can work steadily on one project for hours without becoming bored. They enjoy focusing on a single problem and will keep at it until it is solved.

Taurus makes a great, reliable employee, but it needs to know it's appreciated. If neglected, a Bull will hide its hurt feelings until they become unbearable. Then he or she may just walk out, leaving the boss to wonder what went wrong. One hint: The type of appreciation the Bull likes best is the kind it can take to the bank. Raises and bonuses will keep Taurus happier than all the testimonials and "employee of the month" awards in the world.

Pastimes and Play

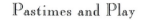

Taurus is not the most active of the sun signs. Walking, horseback riding, or slow bicycle riding in the park are preferable to more demanding sports.

Tauruses are also fond of swimming, for they love the feel of water against their skin. Floating around is enough fun for these sun signs. They don't quite see the sense in diving or doing laps.

The favorite pastime of those born under this sign is doing things around the house, especially gardening. Tauruses can spend hours puttering around the yard, cultivating flowers, herbs, and vegetables.

Cooking for friends is an immensely pleasurable activity for Taurus. A murder-mystery dinner game can provide just the right combination of good food and stimulation for the Bull.

To get Taurus out of the house, suggest a quiet dinner at a good restaurant, followed by a concert. Taurus loves good food and good music. To clinch the deal, offer to pay. No Taurus could refuse an invitation like that.

Love Among the Signs

What is attraction? What is love? Throughout the centuries, science has tried and failed to come up with a satisfying explanation for the mysterious connection between two people.

For the astrologer, the answer is clear. The position of the planets at the time of your birth creates a pattern that influences you throughout your lifetime.

When your pattern meets another person's, the two of you might clash or harmonize.

Why this mysterious connection occurs can be explored only by completing charts for both individuals. But even if the chemistry is there, will it be a happy relationship? Will it last? No one can tell for certain.

Every relationship requires give-and-take, and an awareness of the sun sign relationships can help with this process. The sun sign influences conscious behavior. Does your lover catalog the items in the medicine cabinet? Chances are you have a Virgo on your hands. Do you like to spend your weekends running while your lover wants to play Scrabble? This could be an Aries-Gemini combination.

To discover more about your relationship, find out your lover's sun sign and look under the appropriate combination. You may learn things you had never even suspected.

Taurus with Aries

(March 21–April 20)

A s the Bull plods steadily toward
the next meadow, along comes
the Ram, skipping, jumping,
and running circles around the slower
Bull.

Yet playful Aries has much in common with Taurus. They are headed in
the same direction, and neither will let
anything get in its way. Of course,
they'll take different paths: The Bull

moves best on a level plain, while the Ram prefers a mountain trail. But when they reach their common destination, they'll be in good company.

Taurus and Aries both possess a good sense of humor and are giving, generous people. Aries is a little more generous with cash (Taurus hates to waste money or time) though also more likely to get distracted in the very act of giving. Taurus will listen to any sad-sack story with the patience of a bartender.

Although both signs are stubborn, they usually can work things out. Aries can throw tantrums if thwarted. Taurus will stand firm as well, but not as loudly as the Ram. The Bull will win an argument by appearing to give in. Once Aries thinks it's won, it's liable to turn around and concede every point.

Arguments are not likely to crop up often (good-natured Taurus sees to that), and these two can be a positive influence on each other. Just having the happy-go-lucky Ram around puts a twinkle in Taurus's eye. And Aries benefits from the Bull's stable earth element—Taurus can actually help make some of Aries' wild dreams come true.

These two signs make particularly good business partners. Aries is terrific at hatching and selling ideas, while Taurus's strength is execution. Taurus is also a good money manager and should probably be put in charge of the checkbook. Aries is likely to spend the whole account on a shipload of exotic hats.

Lovemaking between these signs is good. Aries' love of experimentation keeps Taurus interested. And the Bull's lovemaking is a powerful, sensuous experience for the passionate Ram.

This relationship is so successful that there may be a temptation to take it for granted. Neither Aries nor Taurus will ever allow itself to be ignored. Care should be taken to set aside special time together, or the Ram and Bull may suddenly find themselves heading in opposite directions.

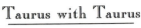

Taurus with Taurus

(April 21–May 21)

When two Bulls get together, they have the strength to move mountains. They have the persistence to cross the barren plains into the golden West. They also have the capacity to drive each other crazy!

Two same signs will instinctively understand each other's concerns and goals. But they also can reinforce each other's bad habits and vices.

Tauruses have only two real vices: stubbornness and jealousy. (Some people count laziness as a third vice, but that's not quite accurate. Bulls are simply very patient people who wait for the world to come to them, rather than rushing out to meet it.)

However, Taurus is justly famous for its stubbornness. Imagine these two mighty oxen yoked together. As long as they remain on the same path, they can move a heavy load. But what if one wants to go east and the other west? They'll never get anywhere. They need to agree on common goals or at least get out of each other's way.

As for jealousy, Taurus has a very

possessive nature. The basic desire of the Bull is to own things—and that includes people. The thought of someone else "borrowing" one of its possessions drives the Bull to rage, and two Bulls mean double trouble. Constant affection and attention can keep these jealous moods from occurring. The Bull just needs to know that it is the most important part of your life.

On the positive side, both Bulls will want a solid and comfortable home, probably with a lush green lawn, lots of flowers, and a vegetable garden. The kitchen will be large and well stocked; the furniture will be practical and built for comfort; and the car in the garage will be unpretentious and economical. For fun, these two will delight in giving intimate dinner parties for a small circle of special friends.

If this couple works together, it will be in a solid, well-established business that provides a steady income and good benefits. And it likely will be located outside the house. To Taurus, home is home, not to be confused with anything else.

In love, as with everything else, these two are straightforward and sensual. Their style may seem less than inspired to other sun signs, but what others may view as boring, the Bull experiences as comforting. And life with these two can be very comfortable indeed.

Taurus with Gemini

(May 22–June 21)

I t's easy for Taurus to fall under the spell of charming Gemini. But Gemini is all flash and mirrors. Sooner or later, when the truth is revealed, Taurus will likely end up feeling cheated.

Geminis aren't liars; they just play with the truth. Their ruler is Mercury, the Roman messenger god who protected merchants, actors, thieves, and others who lived by their wits. Those born under this sign are blessed with too much cleverness for their own good.

Taurus prefers all things plain and sensible. Gemini goes for the big and showy. At the circus, Taurus orders a corn dog; Gemini opts for cotton candy. Such different tastes could be a real stumbling block for these two.

All the same, there is an attraction here. Gemini is the next sign of the zodiac following Taurus, and often a sun sign secretly desires some of the qualities of those next on the wheel. For example, Taurus would like to be as carefree as Gemini seems to be but is unable to give up any security—the price of that freedom.

Although Geminis are bewitching and clever, Tauruses don't trust them, and eventually the Bull will tire of that famous Gemini charm. One can't live on charm or put it in the bank. And Taurus isn't interested in anything that it can't see, touch, taste, feel, or hear.

Gemini is likely to find Taurus pretty uninteresting after a while, too. Tauruses have a natural artistic ability and often draw, make crafts, play music, or sing, even if their nine-to-five job is filing invoices. Gemini is contemptuous of amateur artists, and if something isn't professional quality, the twin sign isn't interested. Sitting through an evening of community theater, even if one's lover

is playing the lead, is Gemini's idea of hell.

In the bedroom, these two are miles apart. Gemini's constant role-playing is confusing to Taurus. One day Gemini is mischievous, the next, dynamic. Geminis thrive on variety and change, so sex with steady Taurus can quickly become a divisive issue. Successful lovemaking for these two will be a continual challenge.

Friendship might be a better bet. An occasional fling with a Gemini could be quite enjoyable for a Taurus. And, once in a while, Gemini might appreciate the company of the slow-but-steady Bull.

Taurus with Cancer

(June 22–July 23)

From the very first there will be an affinity between these two. It may deepen into love, and then Taurus will need to make a permanent commitment to the loving, devoted Crab.

But Taurus should ask itself: "Am I ready to love—unreservedly and unconditionally?" If there are any doubts, Taurus had better think twice because, good or bad, a relationship with Cancer might be all consuming.

Commitment usually is no problem for Taurus, but Cancer's emotional needs might give it pause. Cancer is ruled by the moon, which influences unconscious desires and emotions. The moon is associated with motherhood, and those born under this sign always have strong relationships with their mothers. If they are women, their desire to nurture is overwhelming. If they are men, they are also nurturing, and many unconsciously seek a mate with qualities similar to their mothers'.

So far, so good. Tauruses are naturally protective of those they love and make excellent parents. But Cancer can be so demanding and insecure that even patient Taurus can become exhausted providing constant reassurance of love and loyalty.

Cancer is not doing this to annoy. The Crab simply aches for the security it felt as a baby in its mother's arms. For this reason, home and domestic life are as vital to those born under the sign of Cancer as they are to Taurus. A Taurus-Cancer couple will not be happy until they own a home.

Financial security is also very important to both of them. Neither is a big spender. They often go without gadgets and things that others see as indispensable since Cancer can't bear to let go of money; and for Taurus, material goods are too important to purchase frivolously.

Children will be an important part of their life together. Cancers make caring (although somewhat stifling) parents. Tauruses are more stern, but both are eager to provide stable, supportive environments for their family.

On the whole, Taurus and Cancer are compatible. Their concerns are so similar that a long life together is both possible and desirable. As long as Taurus is prepared to fulfill Cancer's emotional demands, this union can be a lasting one—full of warm affection and love.

Taurus with Leo

(July 24–August 23)

here is something incredibly magnetic about a Leo. Those born under this sign are supremely self-confident, like kings or queens secure in their ability to rule. And who are their subjects? Everyone who submits to the leadership of the Lion. Anyone else is simply exiled, denied citizenship of the kingdom.

Tauruses appear to make very good

48

citizens of Leo–land. Bulls do not mind being governed since they are gentle and patient with the demands of their loved ones. As long as they are given love and affection, Tauruses are faithful and appreciative partners.

This pairing makes for a good business partnership, too, especially when Leo is dominant. Warm, generous Leos make dynamic heads of any business or department. Yet they need employees like Taurus, who can run things profitably and organize the company picnic without breaking into a sweat.

Leo bosses can be overly demanding, but Taurus is up to the challenge. The Bull does, however, need to feel appreciated, preferably through raises and bonuses. And generous Leo will not hesitate to reward exemplary work with the proper amount of cash.

The personal relationship between these two signs is another matter. Putting up with Leo's supreme egotism will strain even a Taurus's patience. Leos are certain they have been placed at the very center of the solar system, like their ruler, the sun, so that everything can revolve around them. A little Leo worship now and then is mandatory.

As one of the most affectionate signs in the zodiac, Taurus can provide all the love and attention Leo craves. Because it accepts love as a natural right, Leo often forgets to appreciate the special love of its spouse or partner.

If the Bull feels that the Lion isn't giving back as much as it gets, Taurus will feel neglected and start brooding. And without enough attention, the Bull's natural tendency toward jealousy can be aroused. This can lead to some of those rare but titanic bursts of temper.

Sexually, the Bull and the Lion should be quite happy together. The Bull adores making love, and the Lion loves being adored. But this idyllic relationship can split asunder unless King or Queen Leo is prepared to treat Taurus like a favored subject.

Taurus with Virgo

(August 24–September 23)

his is an ideal union. Both earth signs, Taurus and Virgo share so many concerns that they seldom have to explain themselves to each other. One knows instinctively what the other is thinking.

Home and family are important to both. Taurus needs to have a home to feel comfortable, and Virgo needs to keep that home in order. Tauruses are fond of children, making very good, if somewhat inflexible, parents. Virgos love children as well and are especially good at nursing sick ones. In matters of discipline, they are even more inflexible than Tauruses.

Both Taurus and Virgo enjoy giving small dinner parties; neither is fond of big crowds. For Taurus, this stems from a sense of reserve. Bulls prefer strong, close relationships with a few people rather than acquaintances with many. For Virgo, the aversion to crowds comes from a desire to control. Virgos need to make sure that everyone is taken care of, and the more people there are, the more there are to worry about.

Virgos can seem exceedingly fussy, fretting over the placement of every vase and warning Taurus not to drop anything while dusting. But the Virgin makes up for it by making a great fuss over the Bull when it's feeling bad.

Because these two earth signs are so practical, arguments over money will be rare. Virgo is more likely than Taurus to part with a dollar but always searches for the best value. Virgo is fully capable of spending twenty dollars on a corkscrew—the perfect corkscrew that will last forever. Virgos do not like to buy things more than once.

One thing that may cause tension in the relationship is Virgo's strong critical streak. For example, Virgo may interpret Taurus's periods of inactivity as laziness and will not be afraid to say so. Virgo's criticism can seem like nagging, but the wise Bull just lets annoying comments bounce right off its tough hide.

The physical relationship should be good between these signs. Virgo, however, may not want to make love as often as the Bull, and that might get a little frustrating. But Taurus's gentle urgings can move the normally shy Virgo to experience uninhibited passion and pleasure.

In bed or out, these two should enjoy an affectionate and rewarding life together.

Taurus with Libra

(September 24–October 23)

The first time these two meet, they might not hit it off. It's not that they won't notice each other. Libra will look gorgeous (most of those born under this sign are extremely attractive and stand out in any crowd). Taurus is also very attractive, if you like the strong, silent type.

But these signs react quite differently in social situations. Libra will mingle and flirt, charming everyone with individual attention. Taurus will most likely be off in a corner with a few close companions, a plate of food, and a glass of wine or beer. Like a butterfly, Libra might alight for a moment in the circle of Taurus's attention, but unless very attracted, the Bull will let Libra fly away. Gadabouts are not for Taurus.

However, if these two spend any time at all together, they'll find that they share similar views on many things. They seek companionship and could make a very compatible couple if Taurus can just persuade Libra to settle down a little bit.

Not that they won't have their differences. For example, Taurus might decide that the couple needs a second car. Libra will probably agree, but then spend hours deciding whether a blue or red car would go better with the color of the house. And since they already own a station wagon, should the second one be an economy or a luxury car? Automatic or standard shift? Libras have to examine all sides of an issue before coming to any conclusion.

Libra, symbolized by the scales, needs to achieve harmony and balance in all things. Harmony (expressed as comfort) is a concern of the Bull as well. But for Taurus it's just a concern; for Libra it can be an obsession.

Libra can become impatient with Taurus's slow pace and confuse the Bull's steadiness with laziness. And Libra's mental gymnastics can prove a maddening distraction to Taurus. Nothing infuriates a Bull like wasted effort. When it gets to be too much, the Bull may exhibit one of those rare but unforgettable Taurean rages.

Like a spinning top that seems at rest while in motion, these two must strike a balance between Taurus's steady nature and Libra's flighty one. Once they find their equilibrium, these two should be able to spin out a lasting relationship based on mutual respect, good humor, and solid affection.

Taurus with Scorpio

(October 24–November 22)

Taurus might be in a church, bar, or bank. It sees a pair of deeply hypnotic eyes. Suddenly, a mist seems to fill the air, the sun is blotted out by clouds, and the Bull is irresistibly drawn into twin pools of water. Taurus has just met a Scorpio.

Those born under the sign of the Scorpion are very magnetic, especially to Taurus. Positioned at opposite ends of the zodiac, each of these signs has qualities the other lacks. Scorpio, for example, has a highly developed sense of intuition, which Taurus does not. Scorpio seems to pull answers out of thin air, while Taurus acquires knowledge slowly, step-by-step, relying on charts, graphs, manuals, dictionaries, and encyclopedias.

This will be far from an easy relationship. Both Scorpio and Taurus are stubborn and possessive, so a few ground rules have to be set from the start.

Taurus has no difficulty with rules. The Bull is normally compliant with any reasonable restriction. The problem is Scorpio. There's no way to know what the rules are with a Scorpion since it will

not make its code of conduct known until its laws have been transgressed. Even
then, Taurus will know that a Scorpion
has been wronged only after it has felt a
punishing sting.

This can be very confusing for Taurus.
The Bull is so straightforward that Scorpio's behavior can seem misleading and
dishonest—even malicious. But Scorpio
conceals its true nature to protect its soft
and sensitive core from being mortally
wounded.

Should the Bull accidentally prick a
sensitive spot, Scorpio will not scream
or hit back. Instead, the Scorpion will
strike a pose of icy indifference while it
goes about getting even.

For any relationship between these two signs to work, each will definitely have to concede a few points. Scorpios will need to direct their powerful emotional energy into positive channels. Bulls will need to show more affection to the jealous and fearful Scorpions.

These two are capable of a long-lasting relationship that is full of heart-thumping desire. However, they are also capable of leading each other through the lower depths of hell. This is not a relationship to enter into lightly.

Taurus with Sagittarius

(November 23–December 21)

As a business relationship, this pairing could be inspired. As a friendship, it could be mutually beneficial. As a love affair, it could be uphill all the way.

The problem is that Taurus and Sagittarius view life in completely different ways. Sagittarius is ruled by Jupiter, a planet of bounteous generosity and good luck. Those born under the sign of the

Archer dance along life's highway, with their heads in the clouds, while Bulls are firmly rooted in the earth.

Tauruses have an inherent need to accumulate material goods—a house, a car or two, a sizable savings account. Sagittarians never worry long about money or possessions. They count on pure luck to see them through, and the maddening thing is, it often does.

Taurus plugs away loyally at a routine nine-to-five job, rarely getting any farther up the ladder to success than the middle, but not wanting to step off the ladder and give up the security it so badly needs.

Meanwhile, Sagittarius is showered

with exotic job offers, even though the Archer may have no experience in these areas. In a nutshell, Taurus hates to move on and Sagittarius hates to stay put.

For Taurus, love is a long-lasting, binding commitment. For Sagittarius, love is one step removed from a handshake. The friendly, flirty ways of the Archer can have the Bull seeing red in no time.

Sexually, these two are not particularly compatible. Taurus loves to take things slowly, including lovemaking. It prefers making love in familiar settings, especially at home, while the Archer enjoys having sex in a hotel, in an outdoor cabin, or on a train.

There are several areas of strain in this relationship, and this is a pity, because Taurus and Sagittarius have so much to offer each other. Taurus provides a stable environment that can shelter the naive Sagittarius and provide for those few times that the famous Jupiter luck runs out. Sagittarius's comic sense and sunny nature warm the Bull's heart. And it wouldn't hurt Taurus to get out of the house once in a while, either.

In a business relationship or friendship, these two can enjoy their unique qualities without the obstruction of jealousy or the burden of a life-long commitment.

Taurus with Capricorn

(December 22–January 20)

I t probably won't be love at first sight. Both Capricorn and Taurus look before they leap. They never buy anything without careful consideration, and they view all relationships as carefully—and practically—as they view everything else.

But the affinity will be there immediately. Since both are earth signs, the Goat and Bull dwell in the realm of the material. Such things as home, money, and possessions are very important to them.

There is one subtle difference—Taurus is interested in *having* things, Capricorn in *acquiring* them. For the Bull, it is enough to own a house. For the Goat, a house is important as a status symbol. But these desires are close enough for both signs to think that they actually share the same goal.

What starts as a friendship or business relationship can easily grow into affection and then love. Capricorns do not trust people easily, especially those who are excessively friendly. But they do trust Taurus. The Goat immediately senses the

Bull's straightforward, no-nonsense nature. The approval of a Bull is valuable to the Goat because it is not given freely.

Sexually, these two can be very compatible. Capricorn may not show affection publicly, but in private it is a fierce and lusty lover. It appreciates the endurance and strength of Taurus as a bedmate. However, when the Bull and Goat fight, the Goat is capable of withholding sex as a punishment, something Taurus would never do.

In general, Capricorn is more vulnerable to the pressures of life than Taurus. Stress at work can keep the Goat from relaxing. Taurus will need to exercise its famous patience when Capricorn is low, because trying to shove a Goat out of depression will only cause it to dig in its heels. Gentle and affectionate good humor will work better. (However, don't try making jokes at Capricorn's expense. Goats can never see the humor in that.)

The biggest danger in this relationship is that Taurus and Capricorn will be so comfortable together that they will forget about the outside world and allow boredom to set in. Because neither sign is particularly good at climbing out of that kind of rut, diverse interests should be cultivated by both partners to ensure a lasting and fulfilling relationship.

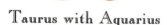

Taurus with Aquarius

(January 21–February 19)

There is much of the genius in Aquarius, and a bit of madness as well. Aquarians live in the future, and because they anticipate the next millennium, they usually display a marked interest in science fiction.

This interest is hard for practical Taurus to grasp. The Bull definitely lives in the present. The future is something to provide for and ensure against, not something to embrace. Bulls live for to-day, not for tomorrow.

In fact, Taurus and Aquarius have almost nothing in common. Aquarius, for example, is a very social sign, interested in all sorts of people, from paupers to royalty. They usually have many acquaintances and few friends. By contrast, Taurus has a few select and deep friendships and does not like to waste energy with strangers. And many of the people Aquarius hangs out with are just plain strange to the Bull.

While Aquarius likes to spend time in coffeehouses, Taurus doesn't see the point of going to a place that doesn't serve solid food. Aquarius likes attending conventions and lectures; Taurus would rather go to a concert. Aquarius usually wants to be on the go, while Taurus prefers to stay home.

Their natures are different, too. Aquarius lacks the patience of Taurus. Bulls handle life's frustrations stoically and gracefully. Aquarians, on the other hand, believe it is their task in life to shake up the established order and agitate for change.

Romance with Aquarius will be very difficult for any Taurus looking for a lasting physical bond. The Bull is possessive and becomes very emotionally involved with his or her partner. Taurus needs a lot of intense affection to relieve the tension of carrying the weight of the world on its broad shoulders. Aquarius is sexually exciting but flighty. Those born under the sign of the Water Bearer have to have freedom—in and out of bed.

Since there is no sun sign affinity between these two signs, an attraction must come from other planets in their individual charts. Even if there is an attraction strong enough to compensate for the basic differences, there will always be tension in the relationship. Still, Taurus could show Aquarius how to be more constant, while the Water Bearer could help the Bull become more comfortable with change—important lessons for both.

Taurus with Pisces

(February 20–March 20)

When they first meet, Pisces may seem incomprehensible to Taurus. The Fish is a slippery creature, constantly swimming in elaborate patterns that look to straightforward Taurus like a lack of direction and a total waste of energy.

Taurus is an earth sign, and earth symbolizes the concrete material world—what we have; what we see; what we taste, touch, and smell. Water symbolizes the emotions—what we feel. It is through immersion of the individual self into this world that true spirituality can be achieved, and this is the goal of Pisces.

"Well," thinks the Bull, "that's all very nice, but someone still has to get dinner on the table." And that sums up the difference between these two: Pisces wants spiritual enlightenment; Taurus wants dinner.

How are they alike? For one thing, neither Taurus nor Pisces is very social. The Bull prefers to remain home, entertaining a few friends. As for Pisces, being with other people too often interferes with those inner voices the Fish is always listening to. But both signs should make the effort to get out more. Left alone, they are inclined to brood. They need others to draw them out.

They are alike in another way. Both need to be careful of overindulgence. The world of illusion created for the Fish by alcohol (or drugs) is so seductive that many Pisces could be in danger of losing touch with reality. For that reason, to put it bluntly (as Taurus would), Pisces is often susceptible to alcoholism and drug abuse.

Taurus needs to moderate its intake of food and drink. Not only will these things add to Taurus's bulk, but they are liable to slow down the slow-moving Bull even further.

Pisces and Taurus are very sensitive lovers. Taurus is especially sensitive to touch, while Pisces has an uncanny ability to detect—and reflect—the emotional state of a lover. While the Fish may be unable to match the Bull in endurance, every act of love between these two will be a truly sensual experience.

This combination can be very good. Taurus can provide Pisces financial stability and a focus on the real world. Meanwhile, the Fish can guide the Bull through a deeply mysterious and utterly fascinating world of fantasy and romance.

The text of this book was set in Bembo
and the display in Caslon Open Face
by Crane Typesetting Service, Inc.,
West Barnstable, Massachusetts.

Book design and illustrations by
JUDITH A. STAGNITTO